IN THE
WOMB
OF GOD

DATE DUE

IN THE
WOMB
OF GOD

Published by Triumph™ Books
Liguori, Missouri
An Imprint of Liguori Publications

Library of Congress Cataloging-in-Publication Data
Schroeder, Celeste Snowber.
  In the womb of God: creative nurturing for the soul / Celeste Snowber Schroeder.
        p.   cm.
    ISBN 0-89243-823-1 (pbk.)
      1. Woman (Christian theology)   2. Schroeder, Celeste Snowber—Family.
3. Pregnant women—Religious life.   4. Motherhood—Religious aspects—Christianity.   5. Spiritual life—Christianity.
I. Title.
BT704.S37   1995
230'.082—dc20   95-11198

For my children

Lucas, Micah, and Caleb.

"Upon you I have learned from my birth;

it was you who took me

from my mother's womb."

Psalm 71:6

Contents

Acknowledgments

M any people have lived this book with me. They have supported, listened, and reflected into my work, sharing the excitement of this book through its various stages. I am exceedingly grateful for my writer friends, Susan McCaslin and Fay Lapka, who listened to each chapter as it was birthed. They also made valuable comments along the way, and gave me the encouragement of midwives. The initial writing of this book took place right before I gave birth to twins and throughout the following year. The birth of this book could not have happened without the friends who supported our family in so many ways in this wonderfully exhausting time. Judi Reimer spent much of her time the first three months of my twins' lives helping out, as well as reading the manuscript. Her presence was a gift. The home group at our former church pragmatically helped our family in so many ways. I also am thankful for the continued love and support from my aunt, Eleanor Sluys.

As this book took shape, many read it and gave me feedback for which I am thankful. Jean Bloomquist and

Luci Shaw made helpful editorial suggestions. Near the
completion of the first draft, Kerry McFarlane Bell gave
me the deep encouragement to keep believing in it.
Stephen Smith was an encouragement and introduced
me to phenomenological writing. Others have also read
this book and made valuable comments: Marcia
Fretheim, Erica Grimm-Vance, Lyle Rebbeck, Sarah
Jamisen, Gail DeLorme, Kathleen Wallace-Deering,
Connie Moker-Wernikowski, Laurie Peterson, and Boelle
Kirby.

I am also grateful to the Sisters at the Cenacle Retreat
House in Vancouver, where I could go for quiet days to
reflect and edit this book. Fran Robinson honored the
process of this writing and was a spiritual support.

I am deeply grateful to my husband, Tom, for his
partnership in life and encouragement in the process of
writing. My children, Micah, Caleb, and Lucas, without
who this book would not exist, I thank for living life so
fully.

I continue to appreciate the entire team at Triumph/
Liguori, particularly Patricia Kossmann, Joan Marlow-
Golan, and Kerstin Erker. I thank Kass Dotterweich, my
editor, for lovingly bringing this work into completion,
and Wendy Barnes, for her creative handling of the
cover and interior design.

I thank God for giving me the privilege of life, for
stopping me in my tracks, so I could attend more fully
to the moments of in-between.

Preface

*I*n the Womb of God is my response to a sacred
invitation to see and hear again, anew—with
physical eyes and ears and with the eyes and ears of
my heart and soul, those senses deeply embedded in
my body. *In the Womb of God* is seeing and listening
to the present—the now—rather than a looking to and
listening for the future. It is ultimately the listening to
our life, in the places where we may have thought
were meaningless, yet are filled with the power of
metaphor which can grab, shake, awe, and mold us.

I was caught by surprise through the birthing of this
book, just as I was caught by surprise through the
birthing of my twin babies. Life had a purposeful and
familiar rhythm, filled with many roles: parent,
spouse, educator, dancer, organizer, friend. None of
this was necessarily bad, of course, yet my attention to
the outer world was beginning to limit the importance
of my inner world. Then, without warning, my
worthwhile and dailiness was interrupted by nothing
more than a mandatory season of solitude. I was

advised to undertake partial bed rest during the last months of my pregnancy. There, in that fertile solitude, I was drawn inwardly, where this book took genesis.

That season of solitude drew me into myself, into deep places of creativity, of gratitude, of God. In those deep places, I began to hear whispers in the womb—in my own womb and in the womb of God. I heard not only the whispers of our babies but the whispers of my own heart. Although I have been on a spiritual journey for a long time, my experience had only illuminated a partial vision of God. I had missed the feminine dimension of God that those whispers gently shared.

The effects of my imposed solitude have remained with me and take shape here. My experience, of course, is not extraordinary; in fact, it's quite ordinary. Many are familiar with this journey of solitude. Jesus modeled it for us many years ago. But because our lives become compacted—a mosaic of beautiful and important things, messy and mundane things—we forget how to listen, truly listen, to the rumblings of the Spirit within. We fail to believe in the rumblings within. And eventually, we cease to act upon the rumblings within.

Somehow, in our own way, we have to learn again to be present, to taste, see, feel, smell the nearness of God: the power of the wind, the beauty of a leaf, the miracle of tiny feet, the delight of a caress, the smell of strawberries, the fullness of tears. These—and so much more—are worlds unto themselves, saturated with God, that greet us each day. Here we listen to the metaphors of our lives and allow God to shape the textures of our days into a holy weaving.

This book was birthed out of those simplicities: the dailiness of attending to birthmaking, artmaking, pondering, struggling, and rejoicing. And with it has come a new way of seeing, a new way of being, and a grateful, grace-filled awareness of the present. Out of my hurried and meaningful life of teaching, dancing, writing, and leading workshops came this gift from God that has transformed my eyes, my heart, and my body. I go into life with a thankfulness to just "be," a deep respect for how God created me and how I am created in God's image.

This book is a series of reflections on seeing and attending to the contemplative in the cracks of life. It is about responding to the voice of God, which soothes, challenges, creates, and re-creates us. It is the common journey that we all share in the womb of God. I offer it as an invitation to awaken to the wonder in your own life.

One

Artmaking and Birthmaking

I am an artist. I am a mother. As both artist and mother, I give myself to the task of artmaking and birthmaking. My art form is dance; my body is the medium in which I create and birth movement.

I am now consumed with creating the space for birthing two babies. I have been instructed by my doctors to radically limit dancing due to the high risk of complications with multiple births. So I wait in the stillness, in the frustration, in the restriction. I move from one creative form to another: from the process of artmaking to birthmaking.

I must hold back so my babies can have a healthy chance; my body must surrender. I become a servant to my body in much the same way my art requires me to serve the discipline of artmaking. As I rest in silence, life is being formed: stomachs, brains, lungs, arms, feet, faces. A miracle is happening in the quiet of the womb-studio. My womb becomes God's studio where the very sinews and bones of human beings are fashioned. It is not like the dance studio to which I go to create—warming up ligaments and muscles, and choreographing movement into dance. Instead, I carry God's studio within me, a constant reminder of God the Creator-Artist.

As I reflect on what the fetus requires for development, growth, and birth, I notice parallels to the creative process: the process of artmaking, dancemaking, or poemmaking. The artist's studio and the womb-studio are places apart, spaces of solitude, where creativity can develop from its embryonic stage to maturity. Artmaking cannot be as awe-filled as the miracle of formation of human life, for only God can design human life. There are similarities to the creative process, however, whether giving birth or making art.

As an artist, for example, I must give myself to the

creative idea and surrender to its process—and this includes solitude. In solitude, the artist in me wrestles with the stuff of artmaking: texture, shape, rhythm, and meter. The discipline of this ongoing solitude nurtures ideas into an incarnational reality where art is eventually birthed, syllable by syllable, movement by movement, pigment layered upon pigment.

In the same way, my babies grow in the quiet solitude of my womb-studio. In the darkness, the fetus is given nourishment from the mother. I, as mother, am required to rest and lie on my back at least four hours a day so my babies will not be born prematurely. Consistent solitude has never been so real to me as during this pregnancy with twins. These babies ask me to surrender to rest; they need solitude just as the artist does.

I, too, find a home in solitude, a home where my creative and spiritual bones are nourished. My solitude teaches me the art of attentiveness: to be present to the buds opening, to my four-year-old son's startling questions, to the beat of my own heart. My eyes need "to see" again so as to fan the flames of creativity. Listening to the miracle of life all around me is just as formative for my art as studying technique. As my physical body expands, my heart and soul expand to the life around me.

Art can be born prematurely, of course. In my rush and urgency to produce art, I have often brought forth forced fruit. My impatience has robbed the art of coming to fruition in its due time, ripened by the daily crafting of ideas, shapes, pigments, or words, allowing it to be birthed in its due time.

I long for my babies to be born in their due time instead of prematurely and with complications. So, I must continue to defy gravity, giving over to my body—which aches to jump, leap, and even contract— to a dance of rest, a place where the pause is more important than the motion.

I am not doing the actual creating in birthmaking. Rather, I become a willing partner with God in giving my body as the space where two babies can grow within my womb. I have sensed God's presence in the creative process, co-creating with me as I make dances or write. Now, during this pregnancy, I experience the creative process through the art of birthmaking, a process that is not only one of glory and joy but is a constant dying to self, moment by moment, day by day as well. Just as my art often has an agenda of its own—not always going where I lead it, breathing its own life into being, defying my immediate agenda for its own—the agenda of my babies precludes my other yearnings and desires.

My most intense physical role is in the hours before birth, when I labor with contractions as the babies ready themselves to be pushed from the womb. Here again I participate in their creation; but it is a participation of pain, a bittersweet experience.

Art can also be painful. It can be painful to pay close attention to all of life, to be fully human, and to give it form. It is a journey in desolation and consolation, as we are honest to our feelings, experiences, and insights, and faithful to bringing them to our art. Our pain can be transformed as we allow it to shape us and find its own texture and shape in art. God-breathed art calls forth honesty and authenticity; it may not always be hopeful, but it is true—true to the pain, true to the joy.

The long labor and the arrival of these tiny infants is just the beginning of the journey of persons being molded into the ongoing image of the Creator. The excursion in parenting begins with the long-term commitment to nurturing, caring for, and feeding my children—physically, emotionally, and spiritually. I participate with God in the process of making living artwork, a human life pulsing with the blood of love.

Newborns continue to be a miracle of God's handiwork of art after they burst from the womb. Their tiny bodies, preciously woven, are on a journey of

change from helpless infants to independent adults.
The fullness of life continues to grow in them in all its
pain and glory.

I, too, am woven day by day into the image of God,
an image woven through my heart and body. God uses
the warp and weft of dailiness to weave my life,
allowing me to partake in the process of lifemaking.
My life is a warp of colored threads. God includes all of
them: grays and blacks, bright reds and earthy
browns, bold blues and burnt oranges, purples and
golds. My task is to be attentive to the Weaver's work,
to discern that each thread of color is necessary for the
mark of God's image throughout the fabric of my life.
God takes the mundane and weaves it into the sacred.
As an artist uses the elements of the earth—clay,
pigment, wood, metals, vocal chords, torsos, and
limbs—so the Divine Artist uses the ordinary events of
life to birth and shape us in a holy weaving.

Two

Birthing

Those weeks toward the end of my pregnancy with our twins seemed to go on forever. I walked and walked—through the park, the mall, the neighborhood, along the beach, in the rain, in the sun—hoping my water would break and the process of birth would begin. My womb felt full, ready to explode with two babies; my frame could not contain the fullness.

Mild contractions came and went, but nothing happened. I waited for what seemed like an eternity, aching to hold my two sons in my arms, to touch their small bodies.

When my labor finally came, it came quickly, with torrents of intense contractions. The whole labor lasted only five hours—remarkable, since labor with my first child was prolonged for thirty-seven hours. But this labor was different because I had prepared for the pain from a place of rest. The long hours of solitude in my last trimester of pregnancy had nourished me with deep emotional and physical reserves. I felt strong and centered inside, the living Christ firmly rooted within my being.

I allowed my breath to center me as I breathed into the pain of contractions. Concentrating on breathing allowed me to be totally present to the pain, making it bearable. Instead of tightening up and resisting the pain, which increases intolerance to contractions, my body could focus its energy on relaxing.

There is something very true and basic about returning to breath. The breath of God is likened to the Spirit. It is God's Spirit which gave forth life in the creation story: the breath of God, the breath of life. As I return to life, I am in the midst of experiencing the breath of God in creating two living beings.

The process of labor became invigorating. Breathing deeply with each contraction, the babies got nearer to breaking into the world. Gradually, their world expanded, from the womb of my body to the womb of our home.

In my previous labor, I had been encouraged to focus outside myself, using a picture on the wall. This time, I decided to focus deep within, eyes closed, centered within, as if diving into a dark ocean. My husband's hand strengthened me as I held it. I experienced again the one-flesh relationship that was wooing our babies from within me. As labor intensified, everything else was blocked out, and I became a world of pain beyond anything I had experienced. Yet at the heart of it, I was exhilarated, calm, and strong. The reality of miracle became sewn in my flesh as I participated in the act of co-creating.

How I wanted to push before the first baby was ready to come out! But I couldn't. When I was ready to go into the delivery room, all the waiting and needless worry concerning the obstetrician favoring a quick Cesarean section were forgotten. Instead, I was ready to push forth the first baby's head from the birth canal without any interventions.

With a joyous gush, the first baby came forth. I was concentrating so intensely on breathing and pushing, it almost seemed a shock. And he was healthy, full of life! The activity in the delivery room rose as the medical team went back and forth attending to Caleb and getting ready for Micah. As for myself, I couldn't behold, watch, enjoy Caleb, for the marathon birthing was not over yet. I could not lose my focus. I had to run the last few miles.

The presence of miracle invaded the delivery room, and immediately after Caleb came out, I thought of the relationship between artmaking and birthmaking; the importance of *embracing* the pain and going within to find my focus in labor was a larger paradigm for my life journey. In the midst of it all, I thought, *this is something I need to ponder in the days to come.* Silently I laughed, realizing that I had just delivered our first twin and my brain had not turned to mush! My creative juices were flowing, and I had to get ready to push out our second baby. For a moment, I had ascended into kairos time and had been suspended in miracle; it seemed a long time. Yet it was only five minutes before the pushing started again, and in another ten minutes, our second precious son was born—and Micah's cries were as healthy as Caleb's.

Everything within me was relieved, as if my pores could breathe for the first time. I had no emotional energy left to push out the afterbirth—all three pounds of it. That was the hardest—and yet it finally passed.

Since then I've longed to write about my experience. It is now four weeks later. It seems as if Micah and Caleb have always been part of our family—certainly they have been with me almost a year, within and without.

Never before has an experience taken on so much spiritual significance for me. Each stage of this birthing

process parallels my spiritual journey—not a journey
of constant spiritual highs, but a journey that
embraces a time of desert waiting. My own pilgrimage
is one of paradox: pushing and waiting, resisting and
embracing, suffering and rejoicing. When do I resist
my life's circumstances, and when do I embrace them?
When do I push, and when do I refrain? Too often I
have found resisting and pushing more natural than
waiting and embracing. The timing in which I want
things to happen in my life is seldom realistic. I want
to get my pain over with, whether dealing with the
death of a loved one, laboring in the creative process
when it isn't working, or waiting for babies to be born.
Through participating in birthmaking, I am discovering
the art of embracing. Instead of breathing with quick
gasps of air, I breathe with a sustained and focused
manner, just as in labor.

I continue to embrace the desert in different ways
and wait in this season of being consume with
caring for our two babies and our four-year-old. My
womb is empty now, and what pressed me to come to
my center and listen to the whispers of God, is now on
the outside. These babies which so preciously formed
my listening heart continue to teach me to wait for the
whispers of the divine in the ordinary. I am now
wooed to another desert of waiting.

Three

The Desert
of In-Between

We perceive deserts as places of solitude, sometimes repelling and other times welcoming. Full of paradox, the desert carries a twofold meaning. It is a place of hardship, but it also creates the climate where cacti bloom, shining their colorful hues amidst sandy earth tones. Deserts speak of monasteries, uncluttered spaces, and deep silences—silences that heal. Deserts speak also of isolation and loneliness, times of being destitute and

forgotten. In the deserts we feel abandoned by those
who love us and expect great things from us; and even
more frightening, we may feel abandoned by God.

I have assumed that deserts usually happen in
solitary places, with few people and generous
portions of time, leaving one ample opportunity to
wrestle along the spiritual journey. But my assumption
is more fiction than fact, for deserts seem to surprise
me at each corner of life.

When my husband and I lived in Saskatchewan, in
the heartland of the Canadian prairies, I often
pondered how we were being formed in a geographical
and spiritual desert as we endured hard times within
pastoral ministry. The prairies remind me of a desert in
their sparse formation; the hard winters strip the
remainder of growth from the land, and white covers
the ground like a forced blanket. Few trees or leafy
forms of vegetation make their home in this land of
open sky and soil.

Looking back I can attest: yes, God was with us in
the desert; manna was given to sustain our weary
hearts. Yet I constantly grumbled. I complained like the
Israelites did. Still, today, I do not recognize when I am
in the next desert. I only feel that I have been
forgotten once again, minimizing the truth that this
place in my journey may be the fuel for my transformation.

Being forgotten: this is the heart of being in the
desert. Does God not care? Did I mess up so
badly that I have to go through this desert discipline
again? When will I come to the promised land where
my dreams (or even God's dreams within me) will
come to birth? I must have been overlooked, at least
for now. I am tempted to compare myself to others,
thinking their lives are taking shape so smoothly, just
as the skilled weaver's hand pulls the weft through the
warp. Oh, how often we have more hope for others
than we have for ourselves.

I am a person who is very tied to geography.
Exterior space often represents a dimension of
my soul. My present place of residence, the suburbs,
reminds me of the ongoing mundaneness and
redundance present in my life. I struggle with the
repetiveness of duties we all must endure: washing the
dishes, buying groceries, cooking meal after meal,
paying bills, changing diaper after diaper, washing
laundry—and more laundry. I long for adventure,
excitement, and mystery. Over and over in this all-
consuming role of parenting three small children, I
encounter the mundane. Although I am one of those
people in the suburbs, I am un-at-home here—
awkward. I do not want to chit-chat about preschool or
weight gain. I long to converse about the essence of
life, poetry and the inner life, God and the twelfth-

century mystics. I am out of place, reminded that this is not only a temporary home but also a home in which I am constantly alone.

As a result, my concept of home is changing. Home is not a geographic place; it is much deeper than that. Home is about being *at home* in our bodies, listening to them, hearing the whispers within and those around us—seeing grace in our midst.

My desert of transformation is the suburbs, not the serene quiet of the monastery. My struggle is to embrace my circumstances. One of the reasons I could embrace the experience of labor and totally throw myself into the process was that I knew it would end, and there would be fruit in the pain. But it's harder to embrace the loneliness I encounter in the suburbs, the constancy of feeling out of sync with the rhythm here. This desert doesn't show its purpose so clearly.

Here lies the pain for me, and the waiting becomes intolerable. I want to know *when* it will be over, *when* I can again embrace the things in life I want to do: writing, dancing, having a bit more freedom.

Is it in the waiting that we are formed? Could the waiting be the soil in which I grow and am nurtured? I suppose the waiting is like a rich compost. When the seed is planted in the compost-enriched soil, it grows and becomes vibrant with life. But compost smells; it is not appealing. This is how I feel about my

life's present desert, and the question I ask is, "Do we
ever leave the desert?"

Jesus seemed to enter the desert again and again,
voluntarily going into the physical desert to be with
God. But he experienced other deserts as well. He was
seldom at home in his surroundings. He knew of a
wider mission than carpentry, but obviously was
attentive to the dailiness of bringing wood and nails
together. His vision was constantly before him, but he
was formed in mundaneness, gaining obedience to
God through dailiness. Details such as these are left
out of the larger picture, for they are inconsequential
in many ways.

We, like Jesus, are formed during the in-between.
Between the depths and the heights is reality, and that
is where we live. This is my desert.

Four

Calling the Child Within

G oing to the park with my son Lucas is an invitation to be a child again. We climb the ladder to the brightly colored fort and make believe we are drinking hot chocolate and Lucas is protecting me from bears. I can run, skip, and swing my legs out into the rain-scented air, and it's perfectly okay—okay because I have permission to be a child, to be childlike, in this place of shalom, this place of play, where I am free from the worry of bombs, starvation, and unemployment. This place is a child's sanctuary filled with the meat of playfulness.

It is intriguing that one of the verbs translated "to dance" in the Hebrew of the Old Testament *sahak* is also translated in some passages as "to play."[1] Play and dance are interconnected at a root or primal level because movement is at the heart of play and at the heart of dance. Although most of us adults have forgotten how to truly play, children invite us to reclaim that delight. And when we allow ourselves to enter a child's world of play, we may actually open ourselves to more formative experiences than all the restrictions we put on ourselves as adults—such as sitting properly and thinking we are too old and mature for such nonsense and games. Could our children be here to teach us what it means to play, to enter the land of imagination where bears and lambs, sun and snow dwell together?

When I go to the park with Lucas, I take a book or my journal, or I simply use the time to dream. While Lucas immerses himself in sand and castles, tractors and trains, I watch and reflect. A poet friend of mine says that poets need "dream time," and I think that this is true of all artists or those who live life poetically, seeing keenly into the crumbs of life.

When it's too damp and cold to sit while Lucas plays, or when all the kids have left the park, and he

wants a playmate, I climb the play equipment with
him, swish down the slide, swing in the air, and
transform the playground into an imaginary land. I
become childlike and free. I feel whole and good. I
forget I'm an adult—involved with my role of nurturer,
giver, and discipliner—and I allow the child to be
brought forth, the child within me who aches to run
and play, dance on the beach, and be abandoned to
the moment. Lucas names the child in me, calling
forth the wonder of a deep-buried joy.

I f we are attentive to its birthings, children's play
can be a gift, drawing forth the lover of life in us.
We can't necessarily command it at our beck and call,
but it will unfold if we are open to the moment of its
magic.

This is the part of parenting that I love and
wholeheartedly enjoy—just being with my children. It
is the domestic tyranny that I struggle with. Yet these
months of motherhood are giving me new eyes; I am
beginning to see that Lucas, Caleb, and Micah are the
bread of angels. My days can often be experienced as
a desert or wilderness, but in the midst I am nourished
by what my children call forth from me. This part of
me would have lain dormant had it not been birthed
through my children.

As parents—and friends—of children, we may take part in birthing our children, but they are here to birth something far more profound in us: the eyes to see as a child again. Jesus said that unless we become like little children, we cannot enter the kingdom of heaven. But it is not easy to see with child's eyes, so we are given the opportunity through our children. We are sent the bread of angels to experience the heart of God.

Five

Easter in the Body

Easter was upon us, resurrection in all its fullness and glory. I went to the church to go over my dance for Easter, a piece to Vivaldi's "Gloria," filled with the resurrection of hope in vigorous jumps and leaps. My son Lucas really wanted to come with me, wearing his lime-green tights and looking forward to dancing in an unencumbered space.

As I went through the choreography, my body was a piece of lead; each leap was a dead weight as my feet came to the ground. I felt contrived and stale, as if only my body was going through the motions. Lucas,

on the other hand, followed me, dancing in and out of
the church with scarves swaying in the wind of his
own motion. His joy and movement were spontaneous
and exuberant. The dance of this child was authentic,
where mine was like putting on an old outfit that did
not fit anymore.

Lucas and I danced together, and then I sat back
and watched him. I quit trying to work out the
snags in my piece; I was just overworking it. My
heart and body could not feel resurrection. I was
not able to conjure it up, no matter how hard I
worked out, rehearsed the piece with the music, or
prayed to be rejuvenated by God's Spirit. I
eventually sat back and enjoyed watching my son's
lively body swing through space with sheer delight.
I thought it was a shame that I would be dancing
on Easter morning and not him.

N ow, Easter has come and gone, and I reflect
on that morning. I could not conjure up the
vitality and energy that was needed for the piece—
such seemed to be the way the resurrection of Christ
was marked on my heart. The central message of the
resurrection shouts out that it is not our own strength
that brings forth the power of the gospel, but the
strength of God. As I approached the dance, my spirit
went reluctantly, knowing that I could not give it my
full energy. I could not embody resurrection and joy,

nor did I feel physically in shape, having given birth to Caleb and Micah four months prior.

In my hesitance, I was again startled with the truth that my gifts and skills are not my own. I could only be willing. I needed to come to a new element of trust—trust that I would have the sustaining concentration and energy to dance and the attentiveness that would allow God to work through me. I was plagued with wondering if I had made a grave mistake, underestimating my limitations. I danced the resurrection of Christ in weakness, just as I danced the passion of Christ in weakness a year ago on Good Friday.

That Easter morning, however, my weakness was transformed into the power of God. I did my preliminary warm-up of both body and soul; my muscles were stretched and my heart became focused on the living Christ. And for a brief few minutes, each time I danced the piece in the three services, my total body was transformed with the renewing fire of God. Ever so briefly, I tasted heaven, and hopefully the body of Christ—the gathered community of believers— tasted it also. They seemed to from their response, but it wasn't because of me; I was willing and I have done years of preparation, but this time I felt hardly prepared. My body still had the marks of weakness; the visible stretch marks on my abdomen echoed the invisible weakness in my body.

So what does it really mean that our gifts are not our own? So often we try to mold our own vision into what God has for us: "I believe I can create a better blueprint than my Creator." It would be so easy to dance when I feel like it, write and teach when I feel like it, or parent when I feel like it. But it does not work that way. Life is marked by attending to gifts in the daily, whether that is warming the muscles or feeding the children. So when there is the opportunity, I must be ready, whether I "feel" like it or not. This is not something that I have just learned or is new to me; rather, it is an old truth. But old truths seem to go stale in our hearts, and we need to learn them over and over again in fresh and remarkable ways.

Ever since I have given birth to twins I feel like everything I do comes with a great sense of limitation. I have glimpsed the amazing perfectionism I still carry within, a perfectionism that has been with me for a very long time. If I couldn't do my best, it wasn't worth doing, so I minimized my own efforts and ultimately my offering to God. Now, in this time, I know that if I cling to my perfectionist standards in exercising my gifts, talents, and skills, I will be crushed under the weight of them. So I choose to do the little I can, but with limitations. Daily I grapple with accepting my mediocrity in teaching, performing, writing, parenting. Never before have I been as aware of my own humanity as I am in this season of life,

feeling so totally human that all I can do is laugh and
begin to take myself less seriously. If I don't, I will
surely be relegated to a life with minimal risk.

Risk. How it beckons us to come, wanting to
mold our very existence. As creatures of
humanity, we are able to do many things well. But
when faced with obstacles, whether they be physical,
mental, or material, we are not as likely to do the job
as we once did. For those of us who are perfectionists,
we find this utterly intolerable; we approve of
ourselves only when we can live up to our own
expectations. Of course, not even a superman or a
superwoman could meet them. And if we do meet our
own high expectations, we then put more expectations
on ourselves to give us another substantial challenge.
It breeds a vicious cycle and hardly gives us an
opportunity to understand the grace of God.

This chapter of my life is surrounded by
limitations. Small as they may be for someone
else, they are big for me. Lack of time, lack of energy,
lack of concentrated mind and body. I am depleted
daily by the demands of giving to two infants and a
four-and-a-half year old. Much of this is a wondrous
experience, but it is one that depletes my emotional
and physical energy and leaves me few resources.
Three small bodies nourishing off mine leaves little

else to utilize my body as an instrument of harmony in dance.

The verses that I have loved for so many years are becoming incarnated within my body: "Power is made perfect in weakness." "Not by might, nor by power, but by my Spirit." "Those who wait for the LORD / shall renew their strength, / they shall mount up with wings like eagles." "But we have this treasure in clay jars, so that it may be made clear that this extraordinary power belongs to God and does not come from us." (See 2 Corinthians 12:9, Zechariah 4:6, Isaiah 40:31, and 2 Corinthians 4:7.) I am only clay and if God is going to use me, it will have to be in an earthenware vessel.

I may always struggle with the balance of being the best I can be for myself and God, and grappling with my limitations. Each season of life will carry its unique drawbacks, and risk will keep beckoning me to its door. But if risk is absent from the life of faith, it isn't a life of faith, and beauty may not materialize from ashes. Easter has reached within my bones; in embracing my humanity, I touched divinity—touching the resurrection as for the first time.

Six

Breath of Wind

My family and I are fortunate enough to enjoy the beauty of full-orbed nature immediately outside our windows. Green cedars and other Northwest trees of elegance tower over the back of our house. This was one of the things that drew me to the house in the first place. So many of the trees in the surrounding area have been cut down to make room for one new house after another, stripping bare this beautiful land of hills, mountains, and fertile color. Fortunately, however, many trees remain. We even have one huge cedar tree towering outside our kitchen window and reaching up to our bedroom above.

Somehow trees have always spoken to me of stability and strength. Firmly grounded in the soil, they are always there. I used to dream of tall trees when I was a child. The lilac tree in my backyard and the crabapple in the front were two of my favorites. And then there was the one I liked to climb, finding my own little tree palace nestled among the branches. I loved to go there to my own little world made out of knots and holes, the trunk draped in New England grays and charcoals.

During those years, I watched the olive tree grow in our yard, the one my mother planted. It was so tiny and fragile; I thought it could never survive and grow in the rugged New England climate, when it was native to countries like Greece. Ah, but it grew—and in fact is still there. But I am not.

I have different trees now, a different life. In some odd way, however, trees remain my sanctuary. When I was on bed rest in the fall, I would lie on my bed and outside would be the great, tall cedar. During that time, I changed day by day: my emotions, my perceptions, and my growing pregnant body. But the cedar, magnificent in its sameness, was there with its splendid branches of forest green rising upward to the heavens.

That fall was a time of going inward, of
rediscovering the beauty of silence and the
nurturing of God in quiet places. My roots were
deepened like never before. Now on the other side,
with hardly any solitude and with constant demands
upon me, I see just how important solitude truly was—
and still is—to feed my weary spirit. I often thought of
the cedar immediately outside the window, standing
tall as an elegant ballet dancer because its roots
gripped the soil deep beneath the fertile surface. I often
wonder how many feet those roots descend. If there
were an earthquake, would the tree stand firm? Only if
its roots were deep, I assume. I suppose this is a well-
worn analogy, comparing our spiritual life to the trees,
roots going deep.

I recently experienced the trees in a remarkable
way: I took notice with new eyes. First, I saw a bird
fly over to the cedar's branches and sit next to another
bird already perched there. This strong cedar of the
Northwest cradled and sheltered these tiny little
sparrows nestled in its arms. It seemed such a
beautiful image of gentleness and strength, something
like coal and diamonds: rough and smooth. It is the
mystery of opposites dwelling together which seems to
touch me the most: lion and lamb; big trees and little
sparrows.

Micah and Caleb were sleeping, Tom had taken Lucas out to do grocery shopping, and there was finally a moment of complete silence. The sun poured into the living room through the French doors and illuminated the entire room. I was invited to just collapse, to restore myself in the few moments that might be given me—and it is always a few. If I don't grab the opportunity completely at the moment, it will be gone. But even five or ten minutes of quiet can restore me. So I allowed my body to sink to the floor, and I thought of all the things I should do—read a book, meditate on Scripture, journal—but I was too tired to do anything but lie there looking out the window.

In that moment of surrender, our garden of trees came alive in a way I rarely see it. When it is windy in Vancouver, it is usually rainy, but the sun peeked its head out, and the wind was gentle and wild. It moved every living thing, revealing subtle shades of green on the leaves' bodies. Their backsides swirled around showing off their darker areas, while the sun playfully illuminated bright segments wavering in the wind. In response to the wind's invitation, every leaf was transformed into glory, dancing in the brilliant afternoon sky. Every inch of tree came alive—flowing, moving, pirouetting—in my little suburban backyard. The wind rose within my own limbs, too, inviting me to dance, yet my body was too weak and listless.

W e cannot see the wind, this invisible agent that causes havoc and beauty in the earth's landscape. But we name it. Its fundamental principle is movement—and this I can relate to, for my language is movement—the language of a dancer. I have often reflected on Jesus comparing the wind to the Spirit in the Gospel of John (3:8). We cannot see the Spirit, but she moves without and within our lives. She enlivens us to the nearness of God, making the branches of our hearts and souls awaken to the living Creator.

As a dancer, I am deeply touched by John's words about the wind and the Spirit. The Spirit's essence is also movement, and when one is a dancer, the language of moving in any form takes on rich significance. The dancer listens to movement and sees movement in everything: in people, in creation, and in God.

I don't ever remember our trees moving with such glistening power as I saw them that afternoon, especially when I was empty of all strength. But it spoke to me of the movement of the Spirit, the all-sovereign, encompassing movement of the Spirit of God in the midst of our world. It is bigger than I and this feels so good, so very good and whole. I am so insignificant—yet it really doesn't matter how weak and insignificant I am, for the Spirit is much greater. She is within me and without; transcendent and

immanent. I want to reread this passage in the Gospel
of John, where Jesus compares the wind to the Spirit,
and meditate on that image with the clear picture of
the wind that I have encountered personally.

I't's odd that we spend so much time looking into
the original intent of the Scriptures, historical
context, or textual comparison—all those elements
that provide us with accurate meaning. Seldom do we
take the area of metaphor seriously. We study the facts
and often overlook the truth that is revealed in the
metaphors. For example, what about the wind speaks
to us of the unique character of the Spirit?

Jesus reminds us of the power of metaphor as he
gave new meaning to ordinary elements: water, bread,
wind, and wine. But to allow metaphor to sink into our
roots, we need to spend time pondering the image.
How does this image manifest itself in life around us?
What are water, bread, wind, and wine to us? How do
these simple and familiar elements picture for us the
reality of the living God within our own tiny world?

I was so ready "to do" something with my few
minutes of time, to do something "productive"
rather than be "reflective." But I was so fully
exhausted, and in some ways paralyzed, that I could
only lie on the floor. Why do I think I need to be in
perpetual motion? Is it so ingrained in our culture, that

we experience a constant drive to do something different, to be something different, to produce instead of reflect? In those moments, I knew that only in reflecting—not by "doing something spiritual"—would my body open to the depths of Jesus' words about the Spirit.

A long time ago a medieval monk said that we must not be afraid of wasting time with God. I first heard this over ten years ago while studying medieval Church history, but it was only in the throws of being a busy mother that I could come to this truth.

Seven

Breast of Consolations

B reast-feeding two babies has become routine; I am no longer amazed that there are two babies feeding at my breasts. Much of my present life revolves around replenishing myself with food, water, and sleep so I can have enough milk for these hungry, beautiful creatures. Through this physical act of intimacy—flesh to flesh, skin to skin—I am invited to see the heart of God. The passage in the Book of Isaiah found in the Old Testament exhorts the people to "nurse and be satisfied / from her consoling breast; that you may drink deeply with delight / from her glorious bosom" (Isaiah 66:11). The Hebrew in this passage is more literally rendered: "For you will *suck* and be satisfied."

As I ponder this metaphor, I am given a glimpse of a God who is tenderly compassionate, intimately involved with my life: breast-feeding at the heart of God. As I watch my babies sucking and delighting in being fed at my breasts, I am drawn into my Maker's presence in much the same way. This image meets me at my deepest point—a vulnerable one—and I am wooed to nurse at the breast of God's consolations.

Few metaphors could describe such physical and emotional intimacy to me, so intrinsic to this metaphor is a feminine, maternal emphasis. God has the capacity to love me in a way that goes beyond all ways of being known. I, as a mother, often tired from the demands of breast-feeding two babies, am reminded that the Creator can be a warm loving mother to me, beckoning me to feed at the breasts of God and be replenished by the milk of God.

I catch only glimpses of this kind of intimacy with God. I ache to be known, loved, and accepted by God in my full nakedness, even in my barrenness. Yet this image of intimacy is also frightening, a picture of extreme vulnerability. As I observe my babies' bodies, I note how they are satisfied and content. Their cries

turn to sighs and musical gurgles—the babble of
angels. Their entire torsos become relaxed in this
tender act of breast-feeding. I, too, breathe a sigh of
relief, a bodily sigh, that they are now content and
feeding on my breast milk.

A s a daughter of God, I am hungry for the
breasts of my Maker and Sustainer—to feed
on spiritual food. I wonder if there are moments when
I, too, must become infantlike to discover the true
nature of the Holy One, allowing myself to be carried
and breast-fed by God. As I slowly let go, I see a part
of God I have seldom experienced, the part of God that
is feminine, nurturing, intimate, tender. I begin to
experience from the inside out a more complete image
of who my Maker is, one that communicates both
strength and tenderness. God is not only judge but
"nurser" of our souls and bodies.

As I experience the feminine parts of God, I give
myself permission to embrace my own femininity with
freshness and clarity. I allow myself to be both strong
and nurturing, firm and gentle. In so many ways
throughout my journey in faith and vocation, my
masculine qualities have been emphasized more than
my feminine ones. I therefore have related to the
metaphors of God as rock, strength, and fortress. But
here, in this place, I embrace my feminine qualities
and own that they are good, earthy, wholesome,

godly, and needed for leadership. I am remade again in the image of God.

E ven though I have broadened my scope of God beyond male gender in recent years, it has only been through living inside the feminine metaphors for God, particularly breast-feeding, that I have glimpsed God as nurturer of my soul and body. The psalmist declares this so fully: "But I have calmed and quieted my soul, / like a weaned child with its mother; / my soul is like the weaned child that is with me" (131:2).

To be stilled and quieted at the breasts of God is the yearning of my heart. I long to be stilled and quieted at God's breast, as still and content as my babies are at the comfort of my breasts. My life is clothed in busyness, yet my interior life craves the quiet of the Transcendent to invade it, to nurse from the breasts of God.

Eight

Tears in God's Flask

Infants cry. It is not unusual; rather, it is the order of day and night. Crying, sleeping, eating, laughing, cooing, and moving are infants' language, the only language they know. Parents learn to discern different types of cries: hunger, exhaustion, pain, or frustration.

Every day my babies cry in one form or another, even though they are usually quite content. Several days ago, however, I was struck by a single glistening tear trickling down Caleb's face, and this one precious tearlet dropping from my son's eye penetrated my core. I was reminded of how the psalmist spoke of God gathering our tears in a bottle, how God records our tears in a scroll (56:8), and my heart was softened and melted. To picture God holding, catching, and cherishing our tears and laments stamps upon my heart an image of a deeply compassionate God.

Tears have been welling within me frequently these days, yet I am too busy to cry. I'm not even sure if something is bothering me, except for a general feeling of being isolated. I am, of course, no stranger to tears. I have shed bowls of tears during my journey in grief over the last several years; in an eight-month span both my parents died. The stripping away of both my mother and father in such a short time brought me into the waters of lament.

Although grief has become familiar to me, my Creator has walked with me through this passage of loss, anguish, anger, loneliness, and eventual peace and rest. My tenderness toward Caleb's tear reminded me of the overwhelming mercy God has had toward my own tears during these past few years. Could God really weep with me as my heart weeps with my son when he is crying, aches when he is aching, and rejoices when he is rejoicing?

Ah, yes. God's love is far greater than a mother-love

or father-love. Yet I find this hard to conceive and
picture within my limited scope of understanding. I
take comfort in the fact, however, that Jesus wept. His
tears mean more to me than any words could ever say.
The Book of Revelation reminds us of the account
when the Master will wipe away every tear from all
eyes, but I am too rooted in this life to imagine the life
to come, although this promise bursts hope in my
heart.

T he material reality of tears remains on my
mind: the way they come with water, cleansing
wounds from within, dropping from deep inside, and
caressing our well-worn faces. A few years ago while I
was on a retreat, I had a picture of God with open
palms extended to a friend's face, waiting to catch her
tears. The hands of God holding humanity's tears: this
beautiful image haunts me. It brings life to the
psalmist's words, that God will catch our tears in a
bottle. I prefer the *New English Bible's* translation: God
will "store every tear in [his] flask." A flask for storing
grief!

The woman in the Gospel account of Luke poured
perfume out of a flask onto Jesus to anoint him (7:36-
50). Actually it was an alabaster jar, but one could call
it a flask. She not only anointed him with expensive
oil but with the oil of her precious tears. As her tears
washed his feet, her grief was truly transformed into

thankfulness and her tears of sadness were turned into tears of joy. Mourning was turned into dancing. The woman's tears became sacred, set apart as a vehicle of worship, an offering to God.

The most poignant aspect of this account is that Jesus did not push the woman away or judge her tears unacceptable. Rather, he received the woman's tears as worship. Her humility was offered as a deep sacrifice of her humanity. Convinced of her own brokenness, her tears wrapped in love were all she could give to Jesus.

Tears are often all I can give to God. When I am depleted of hope and light, my tears become a familiar wave flowing through me during times of grief. I relate to the psalmist's words: "For I eat ashes like bread, / and mingle tears with my drink" (102:9). The Psalms of lament have given me a voice with which to pray, to find tangible expression for my grief: holy grief, wholesome grief, poured out with gut-filled honesty. God allows me the space to grieve, walks with me, and eventually nourishes me with an abiding presence.

The woman's tears on Jesus' feet are not only a powerful historic testimony to Jesus' messiahship but an ongoing symbol of tears being offered to the living God. The compassion that welled within me when my five-month-old son was weeping gives me an earthly glimpse of the compassion God has for me. To be vulnerable is to allow our tears to come through us, to see them as prayer. Praying through our tears we meet our Beloved.

Nine

Consider
the Lilies

L iving artistically is folded into the cloth of
life. It is not tangential to life, but is centered at
the heart and crux of existence. It is not just observed
at the galleries and performances, or for the professional artist, but is for all who want to partake in the
fullness of life. I am grieved when I think of the arts
being relegated to high society, to the few who are
artistically literate, when at one time we all participated in the imaginative life during our childhood.

Unfortunately, the demands of caring for children do
not allow me the privilege to frequent galleries or
performances as I once was so accustomed to doing. In
the last six months, I have gone to the gallery once
and to the ballet once; on both occasions I went with
the class in Christian aesthetics that I was teaching.

My time is also limited with regard to dance;
minimal time is available to go to a studio and
choreograph a dance. I feel fortunate if I can clear out
my living room occasionally and improvise. Perhaps I
focus my creative energy on writing because my
computer is more immediate than driving to a studio to
choreograph and less taxing on my body—and I don't
have to pay for studio space.

A closer look actually reveals that art permeates
my life, not as an observer, but in living
imaginatively, utilizing story, song, dance, texture,
music, and poem to invade the tedium of each day.
The gift of children is that their imaginations are
infectious, drawing new colors into each day, small as
they may be. When the challenge of my day becomes
overwhelming, I yearn for the creative to nourish me
in order to remain whole. The children's imaginations
break through, and in the midst of my full and crazy
day, they invite me to live artistically, to permit the
surprise of sound, dance, and story to wipe the
predictability from my moments. Lucas takes my hand

and we dance to the music of Raffi, a children's entertainer, while Micah plays my father's old red maracas and Caleb plays the rattle. My living room becomes a dance studio.

Some afternoons, paint fills my kitchen—the table, the walls, the floor, and the white chairs spattered pea green. It is intended to be bubble painting—blowing bubbles into the paint with dishwashing liquid, but instead it becomes more of an environmental bubble-green paint all over the entire kitchen.

By the end of those days, when Micah and Caleb have endured alternating bouts of teething, my saving grace is laughter, humor—the gift of comedy, the gift of art. We close these days with the ritual story my husband and I make up about Bozee, a green slug who is really a friend of the family. Later in the evening, when all the kids are asleep, I am utterly exhausted from being up since five-thirty in the morning with breast-feeding, my head still echoing with demands. My body aches with weariness. I go to collapse on my bed and see my flute in its dust-layered case on my closet shelf. The urge overwhelms me to go to the garage and rummage through my old flute music to find the cherished Bach sonatas I used to play so many years ago. I bow to the urge—and play with delight and passion, even though I sound quite rusty and develop sore lips. The sounds of Bach soothe my spirit and body. I come away an hour later refreshed and ready to go to my computer and write.

How easy it is for me to bemoan the fact that my life is so constantly preoccupied with tending a little flock that I have hardly a moment to participate in anything creative and stimulating, much less put my feet up for a few minutes. It seems I often pick up the same journal eight times in a matter of two hours, hoping to read a few pages. The titles, however, are as far as I can get. I know I haven't gotten far when I haven't even read a footnote.

Yet in the midst of my grumbling, my children and I live in creative bursts throughout the day. It isn't something I set out to do intentionally, but in looking back, I see that art is a way of life for me, not an isolated event I engage in. It is part of what Calvin Seerveld calls "the obedient aesthetic life—as natural to our existence as giving our children names and building sandcastles on the beach."[2]

Instead of *viewing* art, I become a child again in this household and *make* art, *make* dances, *make* music. I simply need to learn again the sheer joy of the creative process, a process of surprise and discovery. The paintings or dances that the children and I make are not for sophisticated audiences to view, but they allow us to participate in the wonder of creating. Hopefully these seeds will bear fruit for my children—the fruits of a healthy curiosity, a sense of discovery, and a desire to include imagination in all of learning, whether that be art, science, baseball, or prayer.

I 've been thinking how imagination has been cultivated in my own life. I have spent a lot of time teaching people about art, exposing them to it in one facet or another. But like anything, imagination usually is "caught" more than "taught." *I* caught it. My parents lived life creatively, with imaginative power, seeing the beauty that could be found in the moment. We did not deny our pain and disappointments, but we spent a great deal of time making up songs, stories, and dances. I was often taken to the Guggenheim or the Museum of Fine Arts. My mother would frequently perform her expressive Hindu dances in front of company, each gesture of the hand a complete story in and of itself, each finger a masterpiece of nuanced movement. My father was an artist with humor, allowing us to laugh at our humanity, leaving many memories to laugh about still. It is no wonder that so much of my life continues in the same vein. This was one of the gifts my parents left me. Their own example of living life imaginatively instilled in me a sense of wonder that will never dissipate, only increase.

Living imaginatively is a part of the very
shalom of life: to be whole, to live in the
fullness of texture, metaphor, color, and sound. It is
sewn into our existence. In essence, *shalom* is to take
full delight in our human calling—the calling to enjoy
living before God, to enjoy living in our own physical
surroundings, to enjoy living with our own fellows,
to enjoy life with ourselves.[3]

God's cause in the world concerns the totality of life,
including the mind, heart, imagination, and body.
Taking delight in creation and in physical reality is
inherent in the understanding of shalom. The delight
and wonder of spreading paint on paper, dancing with
children, telling stories, are part of the shalom of life,
the fullness that God has given us in the heart of
living. Truly living imaginatively is not just for "high"
institutions or for those in professional positions in the
arts; it is knitted into our beings.

Jesus told us to consider the lilies of the field.
In his discourse on worry, he invited us to
consider—meditate on—the lilies. The word used for
"consider" in the Greek text is *kataneo*, which includes
within it the meaning "to look at with reflection" or "to
contemplate." Jesus stops us in our hurried pace and
beckons us "to see" and observe in a fresh way. He
tells us to ponder the lilies, the wild beauty of God, not
the trimmed beauty of a well-manicured garden, but

the swaying golds, whites, and greens of the field. Oh, how luscious, if we only took the time to see God's paintbrush sweeping across those wheat golds and earth browns which adorn the face of the land with specks of color and vibrancy.

Jesus used the concept of aesthetic delight to teach us a timeless truth. The call to *shalom* beckons us to consider the lilies of our lives, to make room for them, and possibly to create them in our midst.

Ten

Family as Sanctuary

T he monastery is a place to go apart and be with
God; to drink in the Spirit among the walls of
quiet, to drink deeply of God, to drink in the psalms; to
breathe in rest; to let the sacrament of communion
settle into every sinew; to be nourished on the Word
again and again; to listen more closely. There, God is
in the silence within, waiting to be found. Indeed, God
is on the cross, resurrected, but the wounds remain
within as well. Healed by his wounds—and healed in

the silence—we remember once again the treasure of communing with God. Apart from the bustle, our hurried souls and fragmented bodies become whole again in the sanctuary of the monastery, a place set apart.

This has been my experience of places set apart for seeking God: the retreat, the monastery, the convent. I often think of King's Fold, a welcoming Christian retreat in the mountains outside Calgary where my hunger for solitude was cultivated and satisfied.

Today, I ache for spaces of retreat, but family responsibilities rarely allow for it. It is particularly difficult to go with my husband. It is easier for one of us to take a day or two alone by ourselves.

So, I've pondered my family as sanctuary—as it is so many times, especially when I come home from a day of teaching or giving a workshop. Coming home to the place where I'm known—known with all my faults and frailties, known as broken clay. But I am also known as a beautifully cherished pot, a unique earthenware vase with blue-salt glaze. Tom believes in the beauty I have to give, not in some outward fashionable way, but in the vision of my work. He encourages my dreams, the heart of my life. I need someone to carry them with me, especially in my times of discouragement. Tom also knows my weaknesses more than any other and is even hurt by them. In families, even the healthiest ones, we get hurt. We hurt one another in our humanity and are given a place to learn forgiveness.

In these times, Tom and I live so much in a survival mode that we hardly have time to recognize the gift of each other's presence. I do the same thing with God. I get so busy that I do not recognize the Beloved in my midst. I need to come again and again to my family— that community of friends, children, and spouse—to see the gift of their presence and to let them see the gift of mine: the mire, the clay, and the jewel.

When I find myself longing for a contemplative life in a convent, I remind myself that such a life is not my calling. I need to be nourished and challenged by the rugged intimacy of relational family. Craving each day for tiny morsels with the Divine, my heart and hunger for God remains great. In that hunger, I see that God has placed me in my family for the same reasons someone else may be placed in monastic living. I don't always find being in the roles of mother and wife natural; I am in a place where I am dependent on my need for God, just to be faithful to the small mundane tasks, loving in the tiredness, attending to others' needs, getting outside myself. Looking to the needs of others does not apply just to woman, but equally to husband and father, brother and sister. We are all required to serve one another.

At the heart of parenting is denying self. A friend of mine once said that she saw parenting as a journey in dying to self, a way in which she could enter Christ's journey. She is a mother of four, a gifted choreographer, dancer, and educator, and I respect her spirituality embedded in the daily. Her words and example come back to me now in tangible reality. I think of them often: dying to self. Family is where I learn the core of Jesus' words: "Take up your cross and follow me," "Find yourself by losing yourself," "Love God, love your neighbor...summing up the law."

But so often it is easier to love your neighbor than it is to love your own family. We at least don't have to live with our neighbor, rub shoulders and feet day after day. Yet what closer neighbor can there be than those we live with: roommate, sister, brother, spouse, child, partner, parent. As family, we are beloved neighbors, learning love in the midst of covenant—dying to self.

My husband and I have engraved on our wedding rings the passage from Philippians 2:3-4: "Do nothing from selfish ambition or conceit, but in humility regard others as better than yourselves. Let each of you look not to your own interests, but to the interests of others." So often it is difficult to seek each other's interests, specifically when it means that one of our personal goals must be modified. The

addition of three children, with their physical and
emotional needs, has called out of us a further
commitment, one in which we need the grace of God
to die to ourselves. Sometimes I think it might have
been easier—at least more grandiose—to do the
significant work of the gospel by feeding the five-
thousand or the poorest of the poor in India.

But dying to myself, amidst my family placed in the
suburbs, is what God has brought to me. Home is the
place where I am formed, shaped, and woven—woven
by the warp and weft of ordinary living, attending to
the needs of others: making snacks, playing games
with Lucas, changing diapers, driving Lucas to school,
breast-feeding, carrying babies, wrestling with the
children, paying the bills, making meals, and cleaning
house. On and on and on. All the while I long to go
for a swim, hike a mountain, take a dance class, write
an article, live a life with no interruptions. So I learn
to live in the midst of interruptions, and here I must
die to self, to my self-absorption. If my life with
God, in God, is to deepen, it must do so in the midst
of interruptions, whether that is family, work, or
prayer.

My family is my sanctuary, my monastery. It
is the heart of where God is forming me. I'm
not always clear about how I am being molded, but I
recognize the Potter's hand. When I reread my journal

and reflect on my life, God is interspersed on my soulscape. Poet Luci Shaw has said that, "rereading a journal is like viewing a forest from a helicopter."[4] I see God moving in the midst of my recorded life, where dying to self is daily fare.

I don't find dying to self easy, however; few of us do. In fact, dying to self seems more romantic to me when I think of someone else doing it in some specific Third World context or in monastic living, not in the context of nurturing children. But as I am the one nurturing, I begin to allow God to nurture me through them. I allow myself to be nurtured by God, who becomes a mother and father to me. To see God as mother, as father, is one of the most profound relational aspects of the Holy that I have glimpsed in a long time.

I allow God's caresses to gently touch my weary body, my tired soul in the ordinary. The ordinary: that which I fear most is where I actually find God. Is this not something of what Jesus is telling us about: "Those who find their life will lose it, and those who lose their life for my sake will find it" (Matthew 10:39)? I glimpse a small portion of this truth as I attend to the present in my life—losing myself and then finding myself and finding God. The Holy comes out like sap from a tree: holy sap, death and life in the same space. I lose myself through my family. Totally

absorbed and even sometimes in excruciating pain, I
have to die to myself.

I am one who wants to do big things: big for God,
big for myself. Yet my desire to do the "big" things
can be distorted, for all it does is satisfy my own need to
be meaningful. Instead, God calls me to be little: new
wine in old wineskins; precious oils in earthenware; or
as I would say, a lover of good coffee, freshly ground
Colombian coffee—in camping mugs.

I recently had a profound experience as I knelt to
receive communion in the silence. I took the
small glass communion cup and noted that the rim
was not perfectly shaped—and I knew that same
imperfection within. I was that cup: imperfect, not
completely formed. Yet I knew, too, that the blood of
Christ, the Divine, was forming and shaping me from
the inside out—forgiving me, cleansing me, transform-
ing me.

Our little family is very fragile, as all families are.
All we need to do is look at the families around us to
see that families no longer consist of two parents and
2.5 children. There are all kinds of families, all shapes
and sizes, and they are all imperfect—imperfect and
rough like the communion cup. Yet God dances at the
center of that imperfection; God is there, in and
through each of us, the sanctuary of family.

L isten to the presence of God in others. Allow yourself to be formed in the fire of family, in the fire of dying to your need. And in this process, know that you are blessed by others sacrificing for you, the moments of grace inherent in the mundane.

Eleven

Sea Child

There is a sea child within me; there always has been. It was recently uncovered—again—just as I once uncovered living sea urchins and starfishes from tidal pools and mussels that clung to seaweed laden rocks. The rugged New England coast lives within my pores like the salt air I once breathed every day.

Caleb and Micah were in their stroller sleeping, and Lucas was looking for crabs under the rocks down at the inlet. Certainly not the wild Atlantic Coast, but it is salt water and there is life, however small, in that

polluted inlet. There in that place is the remnant of
ocean, and that is enough for me—for my favorite
place is the untamed ocean, where I am awed by the
wonder of my Maker.

I watched Lucas totally absorbed in finding tiny
crabs, his face turning to glee and astonishment with
each one found. I was taken back to my childhood,
when I would spend day after day in front of my
house on the "back rocks" of the coast, the weathered
rocks that framed the land meeting the sea.

We—my parents and I—called them the "back
rocks." They were our place of sanctuary,
where we would meander on a hot day, swimming
into God-made pools of deep water, or where we would
go during low tide to spend hours climbing along the
rocky shore. It was a world unto its own for me. As I
became older, it became my refuge: a place to think,
cry, ponder, reflect.

As a child, I knew every corner of rock, where one
was jagged and dangerous, or perfectly carved flat so I
could collapse under the warm sun. Hours were spent
there with my family and friends: spring, summer, and
fall. A familiar place to me, it was my home away
from home.

In that place, I would always know if it was high or
low tide by one protruding rock. If I looked out our
front door or living room window and saw the rock's

head of brown algae, I knew it was low tide; if the rock was covered with water, it was high tide, and we could then go swimming in the sheltered deep coves of water.

"Remembering" and "recollecting": this is what my children can give back to me. Watching them, I am reminded of the painful things: what I lacked or how I think things could have been different, better. But if I dare to get inside my children's world—even contemplate it—I am taken back to that classic treasure of my child world, a magical seascape.

I remember the delight of discovery: recovering discovery. Isn't this one of the most remarkable things of childhood? My son Lucas delights in discovering worms, slugs, and bugs. It's a whole new world to him—and I discover the world afresh through his eyes, even if it is the muted hues of a gray-brown moth.

Because our eyes become old, we need child's eyes to see again—to truly, deeply see the things of eternity. This is what children give to us. They give us back the time to see. We often think that as parents, we are the ones who give so much to our children— and to a certain extent this is true. But God allows us to become children, just as Jesus said, by birthing children into our lives, even if they are not our own flesh and blood. We are given new eyes to see through their wonder and virgin sense of discovery. This sense of discovery is what is so delightful about the artmaking process.

One of my favorite things to do when I have the opportunity to go to the ocean is to look for weathered pieces of glass and shells along the beach. When I was a child, I spent countless hours collecting them. Nothing seems so beautiful to me as these objects smoothed by powerful, mighty waves, transformed into new colors and textures. I could walk for an eternity along the beach and find these natural jewels. They really are more beautiful to me than polished diamonds, illuminated with an earthy beauty, simple and elegant. Nature's icons! I can only think of God, the One mightier than the force that created these jewels of the sea.

> *The floods have lifted up, O Lord,*
> *the floods have lifted up their voice;*
> *the floods lift up their roaring.*
> *More majestic than the thunders of mighty waters,*
> *more majestic than the waves of the sea,*
> *majestic on high is the Lord!*
>
> Psalm 93:3-4

I wonder if the seascape where I grew up was more formative than I realized. It was there that I could go apart and discover solitude—the solitude of discovery; listening to my own heart and eventually carving a place for the One whom I truly needed in solitude: God. It was there that I saw my emptiness; I was so little in the vastness of geography. Even as I write this, I can taste the salty air and imagine being perched upon a particular group of rocks. I had to jump over a small passage of water to get there, and once there, I would sit for hours. I would often think that there must be more to life than what I saw, just as there was more to the sea than what I could see. Beneath the gray-green ripple of waves was another world filled with fish, lobsters, sand sharks, and sea life abounding in sundry colors and various species. But it was only there for people who could go beneath the sea.

Of course, I did not find answers there, at least not spiritual answers, but I started to ask the questions. I knew there was something more to life. The restlessness deep within my soul, even as a child, eventually found its home in Christ. God was not in the ocean, but who made this spectacular ocean? It was too beautiful to be an accident.

After my mother died, I went through some of her writings and found an excerpt about the ocean. I don't know if she wrote it herself or jotted it down from somewhere else. In any event, it captures my mother's heart, a heart that captured my own longings.

The sea like a mother to me, sings a lullaby—when calm and smooth—when disturbed, wild, and ravaging, it coincides with all disharmony and struggles that we go through—and someday it will be calm again and sing its lullaby. Like your life always turns back its lullaby. God's personal lullaby to me.

The sea has become my lullaby as well—a lullaby of solitude and discovery. I discover the child within me, the one inside that yearns to see the wonder in nature's icons. Those icons continually point to One Beyond even the Sea, an intimate God who made the sea and me.

Twelve

Glory in the Dust

To give our eyes to our children, eyes that have been saturated with God in all the joys, sorrows, and ups and downs of our days; eyes that cherish beauty, marvel at a leaf, new or fallen; eyes that catch and behold the wonder of life in its pain and mystery, life that allows no control but continually catches us by surprise. This is our challenge.

And to receive new eyes from our children; eyes that dance at the wonder of a Venetian blind opening and closing—something so ordinary to us, but more exciting than the newest toy to a six-month-old; eyes that marvel at toes, so inviting, so exciting. This is our invitation.

To wonder is to praise. From the lips of infants and children, God has ordained praise. Listen to the praise again and marvel at this Creator, the One who knew us in the womb where our frame was intricately woven by an expert Weaver. God has embroidered life and the signature of our Creator is written over all of creation. We only need eyes to see it: newborn eyes, children's eyes.

M y friend has a kaleidoscope she sometimes uses in her counseling practice. She invites her client to look through the kaleidoscope to catch a new perspective. God's Spirit within us is like this kaleidoscope; we need to be attentive to it so we can be transformed with new eyes.

The flexibility in my life has radically diminished. I can't control my babies sleeping, the rain, or our finances. But life with my children is like looking through my friend's kaleidoscope; I am given new eyes—eyes to see; ears to hear. Jesus said if anyone has ears to hear, let that person hear.

S eeing and hearing differently: that is what the presence of God does for us, and that is what my children do for me. God speaks through their tiny voices and their not so tiny voices (my four-year-old can outscream anyone). God is sounded forth even through the babble of babies.

My disposition has always prompted me to want to change my circumstances when I am disillusioned, but I am being given new eyes to see the flickers of glory in the dust, in the moments of the mundane. But my new eyes don't stay fresh for very long without the discipline of solitude. In solitude, I become replenished by God's eyes. Solitude gives me the lens that is needed to look at my life with wonder. Without solitude, my life becomes so crowded that I cannot appreciate the small miracles: the breath of a child, the snowflakes accumulating on the ground, my own seasons of change.

L ife is filled more with the tiny moments than with the grandiose. In solitude I again find my center, my roots. Like the cedar tree outside my window, I dig deep and become at home with myself. I am at peace.

To see the speckles of light in the dust of my life is not a natural process. I am un-at-home with the reality of the daily grind; always longing for adventure, I dream my way out of the mundane. My new eyes need to be infused with God in solitude, breathed on by the Spirit so I may behold the glory in the dust.

Thirteen

Interruptions
of Splendor

The dream has remained with me. I dreamed I was on the ferry—not surprising since the same morning I was planning to take the ferry to Mayne Island, one of the Gulf Islands off the coast of Vancouver. As I looked out the window at the ripple of waves, I became intoxicated with beautiful black and white killer whales diving in and out of the ocean in graceful, power-filled majesty. It was so delicious, so breathtaking. There must have been fifty of them all emerging from mother sea at different times, shining with the glory of creation. I was dazzled and mesmerized by the beauty.

Immediately I wanted to show my son Lucas, who loves sea creatures, especially killer whales. We've read about them, painted them, seen them on educational shows, talked about them, and watched them at the Vancouver Aquarium. My heart spilled over with excitement to share with Lucas this moment of unequaled magnificence on the British Columbia Ferries. When I went to look for Lucas, however, I found him wearing his cycling helmet and riding his bicycle assertively and single-mindedly. He was obviously going somewhere and nothing would get in his way. Although I was close to him and called out to him repeatedly, he rode on with speed and determination. I could not get his attention. I called his name so many times that my voice became hoarse.

Within a short time, my excitement about the whales waned as Lucas refused to respond to my constant beckoning. If he only knew that I wanted to show him the most beautiful scene I had ever beheld, and that I wanted to behold it with him, to see his face light up with awe and wonder. But he never responded, and my heart sank. He would not have the opportunity to see the killer whales leaping with joy in their natural environment.

I woke up at six-fifteen in the morning, realizing that I would have to leave for that very ferry of my dream within the hour. I noticed, too, that sometime during the night, Lucas had crawled into our bed and now lay snuggled against his father; both were sound asleep.

The force of the dream made me sense that there was something in the symbolic image of Lucas failing to listen to me. As I arrived on Mayne Island and looked out onto the cove of blue water caressing the shore of arbutus trees, my dream shouted back to me with significance. Slowly I saw myself directed and determined to go where I want in life, not looking to the left or right, driving myself forward with my own agendas. Sure, they are worthwhile agendas and visions, but they have been interrupted with the birthing of and caring for twins.

It's almost as if these tiny creatures are interruptions of splendor—God's interruptions that have allowed me to truly see the beauty and fullness in the midst of dailiness. My ache to share the beauty of the whales with Lucas is God's ache to let me see—truly *see*—the beauty in my present path, the path of the here and now. And I do not always mean beauty in a pretty or sweet way. Beauty can have dissonance, but it encompasses the breath of life, full with the capacity to cherish being human, to see with love, and to have a deeper appreciation of the present—what author

Gerald May calls appreciation: "the gentle seeing, soft acknowledgment, reverent perception."[5]

God's ache is even beyond my ache for Lucas to partake in the sea wonder, to participate in this moment of incredible beauty. The killer whales were an interruption of splendor, as are my children. Before Micah and Caleb were born I had succinctly planned the next five years: in a year, I would go to Toronto to begin a two-year residency for my Ph.D., and our family would move back to Vancouver when I began working on my dissertation. Tom would take a two-year leave from his counseling position and return after my residency. There was even a plan if I became pregnant; I would postpone my plans for a year and work on reading courses at home. But the demands of caring for twins is not as straightforward as adding another child. Even another child is not straightforward!

I am finding out, however, that it wasn't just my immediate academic plan that was altered. Rather, my core attitude toward life is shifting. I am beginning to see the beauty in the ordinary as I cast gentle eyes toward the present. I am beginning to live in the present, not the future or past. God-given interruptions of splendor have immersed me in the present, and I have been given new eyes—eyes of the heart, not only the mind; eyes to love the shape of a pebble; eyes to ponder a simple breakfast; eyes of gratitude for life. I'm beginning to see more life—and thus more of God—in my own circumstances and relationships. I'm beginning to see life in the pain—and love in the pain.

God speaks all the time, shouting out as I did with Lucas in my dream. God shouts a wholehearted desire to share with me the abundance of life, but I don't always see the interruptions as revealers of truth. Rather, they become invasions and sources of resentment. I always want to get on with my agenda as if it were all so cut and dried. I don't allow the Holy One to catch me off guard, to surprise me with something else. God gives me the opportunity to reveal my heart's desire, but sometimes I don't know it.

I see the wisdom couched in my dream: if I could have convinced Lucas to turn his head and look at the whales, he would have been ecstatic. But he didn't look; he didn't pay attention. Even a cursory glimpse would have invited him to look more intensely—but he didn't. He missed the splendor.

Turning to our interruptions may be more spiritually formative for us than we think. If our eyes can embrace our interruptions, whatever they may be, God may catch us long enough for us to be formed by an interruption of splendor.

We know that all things work together for good for those who love God, who are called according to his purpose.

Romans 8:28

Fourteen

Moving Toward the Feminine Face of God

Imaging God. How do we image the Almighty One, the I AM, the Holy One with many names, the Creator of heaven and earth?

Images of God are ultimately metaphors that describe a relationship and the particularities and nuances of that relationship. Father, Sustainer, Creator, Redeemer, Judge, Warrior, King: all tell us who we are in relation to God.

The metaphors we hear shape our image of who God is
and ultimately shape how we see ourselves. When we
hear only certain metaphors for God, however, we are
robbed of knowing the fullness of God.

The dominant name for God traditionally has
been "Father." For many of us, however, this is
problematic since "father," on the earthly plane, may
connote distance, hardness, or judgment. Fortunately,
this is not my experience. I have a wonderful healing
image from the father I was given on this earth. But in
my quest to know God more deeply, I have searched for
other biblical metaphors that describe God. These are not
as common as "Father," but they are nonetheless
evident in the Judeo-Christian biblical tradition. My
hunger has caused me to embrace imagery and
metaphors for God such as Potter, Midwife, Breasts,
Womb. Images of birth, architect, eagle, and mother hen
allow these images to breathe in me, to gradually
expand into my fingertips.[6]
Several of these images embody a feminine
spirituality, a faith that has not been preached to me
from pulpits, taught in seminary classrooms, or
modeled by my mentors. It is heartening, however, to
find that these metaphors are embedded in the biblical
text, and that they are being recaptured by feminist
theologians, poets, ministers, and scholars.
Of late, I have been inviting these metaphors into

my heart, living with them. I've allowed them to room
with me and enlarge my limited view of God. As a
result, I am being stretched and ultimately named by
God as "cherished one," "sought after," "holy
woman." I am beginning to make friends with my own
feminine characteristics when I not only see but know
God as eagle, midwife, or nurturing mother—a God
who has feminine imagery as well as masculine. I am
made in God's image—male and female—although
year after year I have heard that I am made only in the
image of male. Yet God is not genderless and
impersonal; nor is God male *or* female. Rather, God
has characteristics that are both male and female.

Our image of God is closely interwoven with
our image of ourselves. We need only study
the history of Christian writings to see how gender has
affected theological reflection.

For years I have received the subtle—and not so
subtle—message that to serve as a leader or minister
among God's people, I need to develop my more male
characteristics: aggression, dominance, "the executive,
businessman style," sharp cognitive and rational
faculties. As a result, I have not cherished my innate
gifts of intuitive and imaginative perception. I have not
been able to delight in a more relational, intuitive,
assertive, or creative way of leading: a birthright of
being a woman. There may be a freedom to lead more

creatively, but I continue to receive messages that this approach, in the final analysis, is inferior. And of course, these same messages are given to my male colleagues, robbing them of developing the feminine characteristics within themselves.

K nowing a truth in your head is radically different from understanding it with your heart and body. Even though I have diligently studied the Scriptures and have researched writings from various biblical scholars and theologians on texts concerning biblical equality and gender, it has primarily reached only my intellect. It wasn't until this past year, as I plunged—and have been plunged—into mothering infant twins that feminine metaphors for God have reached not only my intellect but the center of my spirituality. I have had ample opportunity to live inside these metaphors—birthing, breast-feeding, nurturing, and caring for little lives—and I am beginning to see that God truly has a feminine side. I am beginning to experience God's love from this perspective. I have been touched to the core, and my heart has been converted to be tenderly loved by God. The feminine soul that was so crushed within me has been rebirthed and replenished. I am finally owning and delighting in my feminine birthright as I acknowledge that these qualities are valued and cherished by God.

For many years I have been working to introduce people to "bodily prayer," allowing them to experience metaphors for God through their bodies. Subsequently, the vivid truth of the Scriptures pierces a deep place in their lives. All I do is create the space and give permission for them to work; the prayer of their bodies lives within them. I invite people, as a community of faith, to experience God's relationship from the inside out, to know that relationship in the physical body in a way that will extend to the mind and the heart.

A few exercises in bodily prayer focus on the nurturing and gentle qualities of God.[7] One of the exercises I do at the end of a warm-up is an improvisation in being rocked. I ask people to sit on the floor and gently hold their knees up to their chest, hugging their arms around their knees, and rock. In their rocking, they are to meditate upon God rocking them—holding them, rocking their soul and body to the rhythm of the Holy One. While they rock, I often read a few lines from a psalm that expresses God's love or comfort and ask them to reflect upon the psalmist's words.

The impact of this exercise has been profound for me as I have spent the last many months rocking Caleb and Micah or watching my husband rock them. The basic motion of going back and forth is a rhythm of sacredness to babies, a place set apart that is

familiar and warm, a place where little ones grow
content in loving arms.

But this is not just a feminine image—for females as
well as males participate in nurture. Traditionally, of
course, it has been the mother who has provided care
for children. Thankfully, today there are more and
more fathers pursuing an active role in their children's
nurture.

In my rocking I have allowed God to rock me and
the feminine face of God has moved across my spirit. I
often find that people doing this exercise want to
remain in the presence of the Anointed One rocking
them. This is an exercise in embodied prayer that
anyone can do to begin physically and spiritually to be
rocked in the bosom of God.

The other exercise I do is called the "Potter and
the Clay." Each person takes a turn being the
potter and then the clay. The clay is to be a simple
lump, responding to being molded. The potter molds
the body of the clay into another position, gently
moving the parts to a sculpted position he or she
desires. In this simple exercise people discover
countless things about God. They experience how
gentle the Potter is with them, even though the new
position is often uncomfortable. But isn't this so often
the case when the Potter brings transformation into
our lives? It is risky and uncomfortable. Each time I

participate in this exercise with people in workshops, I rediscover the Holy One as Gentle Creator, one who is approachable and nurturing. I see the feminine face of God and part of me is healed.

Recently I've seen a connection between these exercises and experiencing a part of God which is often hidden. This is the part of God that is associated more with a feminine spirituality than a masculine spirituality. It is the part of God that has been sadly neglected in the faith experience of the Church. Not only must we reclaim metaphors for God that have been neglected in our biblical history but we need to find ways to live in them. Embodying these metaphors in our torsos, fingers, shoulders, and chests startles us into knowing the fullness of who God is.

I am delighted and overwhelmed by knowing God in greater depth: male and female, strong and gentle, rational and intuitive. I am beginning to see God through a wide-angle lens; my limited focus is being transformed.

Fifteen

Pushing the Boundaries

One evening as I walked behind the motel where our family was staying, I looked out across a pasture of cows, grass, and mountains peeking over the rural fields. My eyes gazed upon the particulars: the clusters of mustard-green weeds and wild lavender flowers and thistles. They were scattered by the side of the road peering over the concrete, not afraid to invade anyone's space. Weeds, flowers, and grass grew side by side in this land, lovely and fierce with a touch of the wild and unpredictable. It was just a spot of country field in the interior of British

Columbia, but it refreshed me. We had been driving for eight hours with three kids in the car.

This parcel of landscape was radically different than the planned landscaping of the suburbs: cranberry begonias carefully placed next to the geraniums—red, orange, red, orange—a perfect plan echoing people's seemingly perfect lives. So different than the open field: dots of lavender and green overflowing, hay in between, with cow dung pouring through the scented wild flowers. Everything all mixed together; it was so appealing to me in its mixed beauty. It became a metaphor for life more than the carefully planned garden.

The deep things of life cannot be planned or controlled; we must move through them. Birth, falling in love, pregnancy, sorrow, earthquakes, conversion, or death are seldom planned. We can plan almost everything in our lives, but the things that truly hold the most meaning are often unpredictable. They can be interruptions of splendor or interruptions of agony.

The manicured, well-cared-for garden is breathtaking no doubt, but as I gaze upon each house in the suburbs with its polished yard appearing so well-kept and perfect, I often think about what is on the inside. The outer appearance conveys order and control, yet I know the interior is often filled with something else.

People's lives are broken, cracked like fragile eggs behind the outer veneer. The beauty of the open field—bare and humble—has an attraction that any manicured garden could never achieve. Organically beautiful!

The presumptuousness of the suburbs disturbs me, the preciseness of each lawn, shrub, and tree. What is on the outside is not on the inside; there is a superficiality that I long to pierce. Could it be that it serves as a larger metaphor for boundaries in my life? I'm bone-tired of boundaries—boundaries of the Church in particular, where I am constantly forced into a role that is unsuitable to me; boundaries of expectations. It is painful to have fire in your bones to preach God's Word and yet be relegated to the background, particularly when you have more theological training than some of the male pastors! Boundaries are good things, but at times only in pushing them do we grow.

This past year has been a pushing of my own boundaries—and God's. I don't mean that God is not concerned with limits or ethical choices, but I have had not only God in the box of my own limited boundaries but myself as well. I have assumed God's boundaries for me are what others' boundaries are for me, yet the two are radically opposed. Jesus was always pushing the boundaries: liberating women, talking to the oppressed and the outcast, healing on the Sabbath. He was constantly going against the book. As I allow my boundaries to be defined—and limited—by others, I tend to place others in boxes, though I loathe for people to do that to me.

My spiritual director recently said that the scales were falling off my eyes, and I believe that's true. I am truly experiencing this in small ways—being pushed beyond the role of traditional mother/artist/scholar. I don't fit any patterns—and it is remarkably refreshing.

Growing spiritually is pushing beyond the boundaries we put on ourselves: how much we think we can love, be present to life, or be transformed by the Spirit. God pushes our manicured gardens—our attitudes toward ourselves—and replaces them with a wild country garden dotted with lavender and sprayed with thick vegetation. The fertile imagination of God replaces our limited understanding.

Push Lord, yes. Push our boundaries, but with care!

Sixteen

The Holy Wound

The stabs of loneliness come upon me like birth pangs, rushing through my body, reminding me that ultimately I walk alone in many things. I am learning to transform loneliness into solitude, but I also feel a different kind of loneliness: isolation. The process of writing seems to be inherently lonely, especially when the writing is unsolicited, yet I know it must continue. Breathing within me, nothing can stop it from being birthed. Even in the most difficult situation the words must come out.

Loneliness wells up within me, and I cannot go on. I

have to write out my struggles, record them, somehow
make sense of it all. But I suppose that is the burden,
the mystery; there is no sense to them. How can I
make sense of a loneliness that I feel shouldn't be
there, especially when I look at my life situation? I
have a wonderful spouse, a soul mate with whom I
can share my most intimate thoughts. I delight in our
children and close friends and artists who nourish my
creative side. But most days I am alone, and it is only
in spurts that I share quality times of companionship.

L oneliness is deep, too deep for words, coming
from a place within my being where nothing
seems to reach. Is it the human dilemma? Do I need to
embrace this deep empty place, accept it as part of the
fabric of life? Is it necessary for my art? These are the
questions I keep asking over and over again, questions
that plague my days. Is the isolation that I feel
necessary for me to create? I know solitude is
necessary, but that is very different. Solitude is
pregnant silence, an invited aloneness. Isolation is an
intruder, coming at unexpected times, shouting loudly
in the caves of my soul.

Could that deep ache of loneliness be the hole which
can be filled by God alone? Is it my wound waiting for
the Spirit? my humanity that cries out for divinity?
Does it operate in the same way my stomach does
when it is hungry? My physical hunger reminds me

that I must nourish myself with vitamins and nutrients; thankfully it takes the shape of delicious edibles as well. I can actually receive pleasure from giving my body sustenance. Is my loneliness actually my ache for God? Maybe I misunderstand the nature of it, thinking its presence is caused by certain circumstances, instead of recognizing an inner hunger that I will always live with. At any rate, I must be honest: I do not like it and secretly hope it will finally go away.

I was sharing this with a friend the other day, and he said he has experienced this loneliness all his life. I have too. Maybe I need to meet it face to face and give it permission to be there. Maybe I can be full and lonely at the same time. Again, paradox meets me, brushing up against everything I do. Loneliness reminds me that I am not of this world. I belong to God. I will always have an ache, a holy wound which only the Beloved can fill.

But it is not as simple as saying, "I ache and God will fill it, so loneliness won't be there." I can experience the phenomenon of being lonely and still be filled by God. My life is pressed into the Holy, becoming a symbol and a sacrament, a reminder of my need for communion with God.

I have spent years trying to rationalize and explain my loneliness—but now, here, I know that I can no longer do this. I still may not like its ache, but I am challenged to come to a deeper acceptance of it. I am still perplexed over whether it is part and parcel of artmaking; isolation pushes me to create, to find meaning in the emptiness and in the fullness. The intensity in which I live is so great at times that I feel compelled to share it through my art. I cannot contain it within my body, and it must be fleshed out in dance and words.

One of my artist friends felt that I needed to attend to writing a chapter on loneliness or isolation, but I wanted to disregard her suggestion. Yet the mere thought made me own the very thing that I wanted to escape. Perhaps, however, her intuition was right. Here in the midst of loneliness, it is a good friend who challenges me to meet my own ache face to face.

We can read our lives by our aches more than anything else. Just as our physical aches reveal something, our spiritual, emotional, and intellectual aches reveal another reality. Unfortunately, it is not as easy as going to the doctor and taking a pill or antibiotic so it will disappear. Some aches are with us forever.

I can't seem to get out of my mind the accounts in Latin America of hundreds of children and mothers

being killed, their bones being unearthed. What pain
that must be for a mother to hear her children
screaming for her as they meet their death. What
savage pain remains to those who are left behind. This
is a loneliness that goes beyond anything I have ever
experienced; a deep letting go of womb-love. Mine is
pale in comparison. I ache with those children and
mothers.

I'd like to think that my loneliness will be my
lifetime reminder that I live in paradox, the
paradox of my eternal home in God and my home on
earth right now. They come together, but they are
apart. They both live within me: clay and jewels,
earthenware and porcelain, lion and lamb, male and
female. As I am invited to partake more of divinity
along my journey, I am immersed more in humanity.
Spirituality is not ethereal, but real, embedded in earth,
getting mud on our face. Spirituality is a messy
enterprise.

Underneath all of this, the ache of loneliness
reminds me that I am on a journey, a very precious
journey that beckons me to transformation. But
transformation comes in the midst of laughter and
tears, fullness and emptiness, worship and play,
loneliness and communion. God meets me in each,
and it is in the meeting that I am made whole.

Seventeen

Resting on
Eagle's Wings

I had just stretched out for a nap when I heard echoes of children's voices, strong but muffled in the background, as recess began at the elementary school near my home. I remembered hearing children's voices from my childhood home—the kids playing at the nearby beach as if they were all calling to me in unison, "Come and play, Celeste!" Their sounds made music from afar, inviting me to the wonder of digging holes in the mud, dipping in the salt sea, and making

castles and tunnels in the sand. I would wait an
eternity for my mother to finish her housework so we
could enter this playland of nature; fresh breezes and
soft pliable sand were better than any of my store-
bought toys.

I remember waiting for low tide as if it were a long-
awaited holiday. The sandbars emerged at low tide.
Little lands all to themselves, they would carve pools
of warm New England water, just the right size for
play and imagination. Totally absorbed in the magical
world at the sandbar, my soul and body yearned for
the beach each summer. The sandbar would transform
itself as it became covered with the waters of high tide;
I could then swim over my head and enter the
adventure of finding the sandbar, almost like
discovering a boat to dive off, a haven of rest, or a
strong rock for refuge. Standing on my rock of sand, I
had the opportunity to rest my body from my swim
and dive in and out of the cold deep ocean.

Havens of rest and refuge are what I yearn for.
Where are the sandbars in my life now,
where I delight in play? Somehow there must be a
deep relationship between play and entering refuge,
refuge of wonder and creativity, a place to be totally
absorbed in being free. I think of how Lucas and I
make our homemade fort; it's really a sheet draped
over an old couch that folds out to a sleeping bed. In

these moments, the dining room becomes a place for
play, as all furniture is cleared out except for our
couch-fort, ideal for climbing through, hiding in,
jumping on, sliding over, and bringing all three
children into a wonderful suburban cave, a haven of
rest in our busy lives.

W hen I put a sheet over one side that rests
high upon the bookcase, we have a portable
tent. Micah and Caleb love it, poking the sheet as if it
were a bellowing cloud, laughing after every poke.
Lucas rolls up in his sleeping bag and cozily snuggles
like a little worm in a blue bag. I, too, enjoy resting my
weary body in our homemade cave.

It is amazing how changing the formation of space
transforms an ordinary late afternoon day. Lucas and I
forget how hungry we are. Instead, we enter a
different kind of time—the time of kairos, one that
children are naturally given to. I am far more often in
chronos time: measuring my minutes and days. But
when I enter play and prayer, the wonder of creating
or lovemaking, I again enter kairos, the eternal
present. This is the ongoing gift of my children; I am
given permission to enter kairos.

C hildren love tents and caves, the feeling of
being under the sheets with flashlights. Such
places are a home away from home, a safe refuge.

Sometimes I wonder if that is why camping has such an appeal, providing a haven of rest in the wild. When we take refuge in our couch-fort, I often entertain a brief time of meditation on the metaphor of God as an eagle. In my prayer, I take refuge in and on the wings of my Maker. In this image of complete protection, I become transformed in much the same way as I enter our homemade cave. I am safe, accepted; I rest in the shadow of the wings of the Almighty.

As I meditate on the metaphor of the eagle found in the passages of Isaiah in the Old Testament, I am struck by the fact that the eagle is most likely a female, for the female is the stronger of the gender and protects and cares for her young.[8] This image of the strong eagle soaring across the weather-beaten sky, protecting and nurturing her young, is liberating for me. I am a strong woman, but I also spend lots of time nurturing. I need images of being feminine, images of strength. This season of my life particularly draws me to this image, but I believe it is an image I need for the endurance of my life on earth. To experience the refuge of my God's wings, embracing my aching bones and weary spirit, transfuses strength into me. I am born anew, replenished by the Holy Spirit living within. The passage in Isaiah, "those who wait upon the Lord will mount up with eagle's wings," becomes fused to my flesh (40:31). It is not just beautiful Scripture; it is a fertile reality.

I rise again with strong wings in the process of taking refuge in my Maker, the eagle of love, whose nest is a haven where I can go in my few moments of alone time or in my busyness. The image comes back to me as I enter the world of play with my children. As simple as putting a sheet on my couch for a fort or a tent is going to the wings of God.

In my intensity of mothering, I need to be mothered by the Holy One. If I am not, I surely will shrivel up inside. I experience from inside out the God of refuge, and I long to daily come and hide in God's wings of love. God is the refuge in my life, the haven of rest and replenishment, the place where I receive a spiritual transfusion so I can again enter the intensity of dailiness.

Eighteen

In the Womb
of God

*I*n *the Womb of God* is in its last trimester, ready
to come forth with the pangs of labor. It reminds
me so well of the last few weeks of pregnancy with
Micah and Caleb. I kept experiencing false labor,
knowing my babies must burst forth from my large
swollen womb, but my labor never really amounted to
anything, at least not to an immediate trip to the
hospital. I kept walking, hoping the walking would
precipitate labor, but labor didn't begin for many

weeks. Although I had hoped that our babies would come early, I respected my doctor's and obstetrician's caution regarding the high risk of prematurity with multiple births. I quit lecturing, went on bed rest, and paid constant attention to the demands of my body. This is what I wanted and waited for, a healthy delivery that would go to full term, but I felt too full, too ready to come forth with life. If these babies stayed much longer, they would certainly need to be induced. I physically could not bear it any longer, hardly being able to sleep, walk, or sustain any position that was comfortable. I ached for these babies to be on the outside.

The end of this book seems to parallel the experience of my last trimester. For months I have sensed the last chapter was about to be birthed, anticipating the direction and content in the moments of my days. Yet it cannot be drawn forth from my womb-studio. I have whispers of it, but no loud voices. Even now, here at the computer, I feel the pangs of art-labor finally flowing. When Caleb accidentally rebooted the computer while meandering in my office, I lost a page of work—one of those pages that writers wait for. I am wondering if this last chapter has to be "physically induced."

As I was reflecting on this, I pondered what actually was needed to induce this chapter. I began to realize that I was not really sure that I wanted this book to be born—for its birth will mean the "end" of something I have delighted in for so long. It has been a process where I again have found my center and have made meaning of the canvas of my life. I want it to go on forever, at least the joy of reflecting and writing. And undoubtedly, this could go on. I also know that now is the time to let go, to release these pages from my hands, to be scrutinized, chopped, criticized, edited, and ultimately read by many I don't know, and even more unsettling, by those I do know.

For the first time I really considered what it might be like to carry a child for nine months, and after all that time of bonding and loving this child within, to let her go. No wonder so many teenage mothers end up keeping their babies! The process of letting go is more painful than all the responsibilities of raising a child in an economically unstable situation. The birth mother provides a warm womb in which this baby is nourished, sustained, and transformed into a tiny creature with hands, feet, heart, and soul. She is invited to participate in the act of co-creating, forming a deep bond with this life, yet she must relinquish her passion to hold and nurture this child on the outside, to take part in the wonder of ongoing formation of her daughter or son. To let go of a baby after carrying it to full term is an act of love—love that hurts. But often, only in letting go does this child have a chance to develop into who she is meant to become.

I must come to terms with letting go of my own words before I can let this last chapter come through my heart and fingers. It seems presumptuous to anticipate letting go when I do not know what the outcome of this writing will be. But I must remember that I do not own my words; they are ultimately gifts from the One who gave us words, the supreme Wordgiver, the Birthmaker, the Artmaker.

Letting go is an illusory process. It is not as if, in one odd moment, I say, "I let go," and that is it. Rather, it is more like a slow process of pulling, taking, grasping, and slipping. Letting go is a process, not a one time decision. I let go and take back; I let go and grasp; I let go and slip; and eventually, when I don't realize it, I have let go into the One who carries me on eagle's wings. Even in letting go, I am being molded and formed by the One who let me go to risk, to trust, to love. Hearing the whispers of God, I am nudged to lose what has taken flight in my own heart, so others may receive.

Again the parallel with children and art is very real to me. We must let go of children, and we must let go of art. Ultimately it is an act of love. As I let go of my children from my womb, I was invited on a journey of the most complete love of all: womb-love; the love of God.

I have been wooed to the womb of God these last several months. This metaphor of absolute warmth and shelter has permeated my thoughts, meditations, and prayers. Having my womb full with two developing babies pushed me repeatedly to turn my heart toward my body. The demands of birthmaking invited me to rediscover the fullness of solitude—a solitude that was pregnant with a silence as deep and colorful as the ocean floor.

Now solitude comes in smaller portions, but I manage to uncover it in pockets and periodically take a day alone to restore my soul and body at the Cenacle, a retreat house in Vancouver. Those months of solitude while on bed rest enabled me to store a deep reservoir within, almost as a bear regains rest in hibernation. I am still nourished by the well of quiet within me, the place where I commune with Jesus.

My womb is empty now. What I loved and cared for on the inside, I continue to delight in and nurture on the outside. My babies continue to cause me to pay attention to my body. Their physical demands press my body to drink of solitude for my daily nutrients. Even as I finish this sentence, Tom brings Caleb and Micah into my office for a drink of breast milk. As my body continues to give, it also needs to be replenished in the womb of God.

Even though my womb is empty, the reality of the

womb has not left me; it lingers in the remains of my heart with profound meaning. God is not forming life in my womb-studio, but I continue to be formed, fashioned, and present in the womb of God. God's Spirit is pregnant within me. My friend told me once that while swimming she imagined she was swimming in the womb of God. The waters of the pool were analogous to the water that sustains the fetus. A striking image: many people swimming in this huge body of water and possibly only a few recognizing God as the source and giver of life. I thought it was a wonderful way of thinking metaphorically about "being" in the presence of God, being in God's womb.

L iving in the womb of God, caressed by the touch of the Beloved, I am made whole and regain the strength to meet the next moment. As I learn to be present to God in the midst of the dailiness and clutter of my life, I begin to see that I live in the womb of God. God encompasses me as a mother and father caress their unborn child. The child cannot see her parents caressing her, but senses she is loved and known.

God says to the prophet Jeremiah, "Before I formed you in the womb I knew you" (Jeremiah 1:5). God knows us like that, providing womb-love from a gentle and strong Creator. As I constantly nurture children, I yearn to be tenderly and compassionately nurtured by

God. When I experience God's love for me as womb-love, I profoundly enter the compassion of God. I am again named a special and beloved daughter.

I t is not surprising that one of the words in the Old Testament used to convey the deepest kind of mercy and compassion God can have for the Israelites has the same root that is used for womb: *raham.* This word conveys a deep love, akin to the natural bond of a child in the womb.

As a father has compassion (raham) for his children,
so the LORD has compassion for those who fear him.
                                                      Psalm 103:13

Womb-love: this is God's love—a love that no force can break or alter, a strong deep love that is woven with the threads of grace and mercy. I want to live in the kind of love God has for me, letting it seep through my frame, not just cognitively understanding it.

In order for me to more fully participate in the womb of God, being present to God's womb-love for me, I need to surrender to God in the present. But where is God in the midst of my daily life, in the dust and glory? I'm beginning to see that God is easy to miss. It is so easy to form God in my own image rather than be formed in the image of my Creator. Unfortunately, I do not surrender with grace as the leaves do outside my window. Rather, I sometimes need interruptions of splendor to turn my life upside down and arc my heart toward God.

I've been watching those golden maple leaves outside my bedroom window. The tree grows bare; only a cluster of golden-yellow stars remains hanging with their extended stems surrendering to the light, waiting to depart and cascade to the ground. The leaves have their own gestures, and I look with wonder at how much ease they abandon themselves to change.

I particularly notice how translucent the leaves appear as sunlight bathes their bodies. Almost ethereal, they seem to wait with grace as they anticipate letting go. They seem to trust instinctively their season of change and bow with a gesture of surrender to the God who made them.

I do not let go so easily. But in my journey of discovering God's womb-love, I yearn to let go in the Beloved's arms. I yearn to be present to each moment, so I will not miss the beauty of God's womb in which I have my being. I believe God wants to surprise me, and I must become like a child to receive it. Love requires not a one time of becoming, but an ongoing surrender into the womb of God—a womb that is pregnant with the birth pangs of love.

Notes

1. Mayer I. Gruber. "Ten Dance-Derived Expressions in the Hebrew Bible," in Doug Adams and Diane Apostolos-Cappadona, *Dance as Religious Studies* (New York: Crossroad, 1990), 58-59.

2. Calvin Seerveld. *Rainbows for the Fallen World: Aesthetic Life and Artistic Task* (Toronto: Toronto Tuppence Press, 1980), 49-50.

3. For a full development of the concept of *shalom*, see Nicholas Wolterstorff, *Until Justice and Peace Embrace* (Grand Rapids, MI: Eerdmans, 1980) and *Art in Action* (Grand Rapids, MI: Eerdmans, 1980).

4. Luci Shaw. *Life Path: Personal and Spiritual Growth Through Journal Writing* (Portland, OR: Multnomah, 1991), 34.

5. Gerald G. May, M.D. *The Awakened Heart: Living Beyond Addiction* (San Francisco: Harper & Row, 1991), 20.

6. To see the metaphor of God as eagle see Deuteronomy 32:11-12; as mother see Hosea 11:3,8, 13:8, and Isaiah 66:13; birth images and God see Isaiah 42:13, 46:3-4, and James 1:18; God as a mother hen see Matthew 23:37; God as midwife see Psalm 22:9-10.

7. For a detailed explanation of the following exercises see Appendix 1 in Celeste Snowber Schroeder, *Embodied Prayer: Harmonizing Body and Soul* (Liguori, MO: Triumph Books, 1995), 185-204

8. Jane Aldredge Clanton. *In Whose Image? God and Gender* (New York: Crossroad, 1990), 23-24.

About the Author

Celeste Snowber Schroeder is a liturgical dance artist, educator, and writer who focuses her work in the area of spirituality and the body. She periodically teaches at Regent College, Trinity Western University and Pacific Northwest Institute of Spiritual Direction and frequently leads workshops in a variety of settings. She is the author of *Embodied Prayer: Harmonizing Body and Soul*, also published by Triumph. She is currently finishing her Ph.D. at Simon Fraser University and raising her three children with her husband, Tom, near Vancouver, British Columbia.